Emily R Logue

At the Foot of the Mountain

Emily R Logue

At the Foot of the Mountain

ISBN/EAN: 9783337289560

Printed in Europe, USA, Canada, Australia, Japan

Cover: Foto ©Andreas Hilbeck / pixelio.de

More available books at **www.hansebooks.com**

At the Foot of the Mountain

EMILY R. LOGUE

PHILADELPHIA

H. L. KILNER & CO.

Publishers

TO

My Father and Mother

WHOSE PATIENCE, GENTLENESS, AND UNTIRING
SELF-SACRIFICE HAVE MADE THE
B'RIGHTNESS OF OUR
HAPPY HOME.

CONTENTS

	PAGE
THE DAISY	7
PHILADELPHIA	8
BABY	9
THANKSGIVING	11
OUR FAITH AND OUR COUNTRY	13
OUR DEAREST AND BEST WE GIVE UNTO THEE	14
TO LONGFELLOW'S PICTURE	15
TO ST. CATHARINE OF ALEXANDRIA	17
MUSIC	18
IN THE PEACE PAST UNDERSTANDING	21
SIC TRANSIT GLORIA MUNDI	23
THREE FRIENDS OF MINE	25
SYMPATHY	28
HYMN TO ST. CATHARINE	29
REQUIESCAT	30
IN MEMORIAM	31
A PICTURE	32
GREETING TO REV. GERALD P. COGHLAN	35
THE PARTING OF THE WAYS	37
LIGHT	39
ODE FOR THE SILVER JUBILEE OF THE CATHEDRAL T. A. B. SOCIETY	40
MY DARTHEA	42
THE HIGHEST ART	43
TO ALICE	44
ALONE	45
LAST DAYS	46

THE DAISY.

Written for the L. C. C.

Low in the fragrant meadow the sweet, white flowers lie,
Engulfed in the waving grasses like stars in a clouded
  sky;
O purest white! O yellow gold! how great, how wide
  thy scope,
Combining Faith with love of land, our hero, and our
  Pope.
O little flower of innocence! O daisy, fair and bright!
Lowly thou art, yet none could be more precious in our
  sight.
Until the close of earthly life our model thou shalt be,
Modest in worth, in beauty meek, spotless in purity!

Before the sleeping ages wake, Lord, grant that we may
  live
In the innocence of childhood, with the wisdom years
  should give,
And be as Thine own little ones, and worthy our home
  above;
Ne'er shall the tempter conquer 'neath the shield of Thy
  perfect love.

Calvary's Cross was lifted that sin from us might fly!
Let us live for His greater glory, die for Him when we
  die.
Unfettered by the chains of sin may we go to join the
  fold,
Beloved of God, in heaven to share the joy earth cannot
  hold.

7

PHILADELPHIA.

Song of the L. C. C.

Beloved Philadelphia! the clear sunlight falls
Serenely to-day on thy historic walls;
And gladly thy children of freedom's bright days
Unite, Philadelphia, in singing thy praise!
'Mid the Stars and the Stripes to the calm breeze
    unrolled,
Most proudly the blue and the buff we enfold,
With fast-beating hearts that are loyal to thee,
Beloved Philadelphia, the home of the free!

Where calmly to-day, under Freedom's blue sky,
Columbia's fair banners are waving on high,
The hand of oppression was heavily laid,
When we bowed under laws that a tyrant had made.
Then, thou, Philadelphia, with generous hand,
Didst offer thy bravest and best for our land;
No man found thee wanting, and proudly we claim
The City of Brotherly Love as thy name.

To the God of our country, Whom all men obey,
For thee, native city, most humbly we pray
That peace and affection may dwell evermore
In the hearts and the homes of our dear native shore.
May the blessing thy bell pealed a blessing remain
In the land for which heroes were willingly slain.
All honor, all love, and all praise unto thee,
Beloved Philadelphia, the home of the free!

BABY.

The moonlight streams into the room,
　And guided by its light I trace
The outline, all untouched by gloom,
　Of a baby's pure, sweet face.

More dear than life and wealth to me,
　More fair than brilliant charms,
The form I hold so tenderly
　Within my loving arms!

What shall I wish for him to-night?
　For worldly wealth or earthly gain?
Ah! would they make his future bright,
　Or would they only bring him pain?

I know that thorns must always be
　Upon the fairest roses found,
Yet I would try, dear one, for thee
　To learn where thornless ones abound.

I know the little hands that rest
　So quietly on mine to-night,
May be with Heaven's riches blessed
　To lead some wayward heart aright.

These trembling little feet may press
　　Hard roads, which love makes smooth to-day;
These eyes be dim with weariness
　　When youth's clear brightness fades away;

But God's light shines on fair and clear,
　　Though every earthly joy may fleet,
And I may trust HIM without fear
　　To guide the baby's feet.

THANKSGIVING.

Across the dear old church the morning sun
    Falls softly on the heads bowed low in prayer;
On each unhappy and each joyous one,
    Glowing with youth, or worn with age and care.

Far down the aisle, where fitful shadows creep,
    A woman kneels with silver head bent low;
Too worn with sorrow are the eyes to weep
    That gaze, while hurried footsteps come and go,

Upon the shining Cross above the Throne
    Where God is resting, that His children may
Kneel at His altar where He reigns alone,
    And praise His bounty on Thanksgiving Day.

"Father!"—the trembling hands are clasped in prayer,
    A strange light dawns upon the features mild,—
"I thank Thee for the years of loving care
    Which Thou hast given to an unworthy child;

"I thank Thee for the grace which always gave
    Me faith and strength to say, 'Thy Will be done;'
Thy loving grace, which made me calm and brave
    When Thou didst take from me each well-loved one.

"I know that safe from every care and pain
    They rest in Thee, where trials are unknown:
Then, Lord, accept from my poor heart a prayer
    Of thankfulness that through much sorrow I have
        grown

"To love Thee more, and say with each succeeding
    year,
  'Oh! may Thy Holy Name be always blessed;'
To lean on Thee, Who dries the mourner's tear,
  And gives the weary heart eternal rest!"

Lower the silver head was bent, the noon-day sun
  Fell softly on the figure worn and old;
And high in heaven, ere the simple prayer was done,
  A woman's name was marked in shining gold.

OUR FAITH AND OUR COUNTRY.

On primal rock sublimely standing,
    Undaunted by a trace of fear;
Reposing silent, yet commanding—
    Faith of our fathers, holy, dear!
Anew we pledge our trust to thee,
    In union with our love of land
That life-blood shed for liberty
    Has made a nation, free and grand.

Amid the battle's din and roar,
    No braver men than ours e'er fought;
Deep in their hearts a silent prayer
    Of hope, for freedom—dearly bought.
Up to the fair blue sky, its bright stars worn and
        dim,
    Rose proudly the tattered flag—forever free,
Crimson with blood, with powder black and grim.
    Our Faith! Our Country! proudly we
Unite with love 'neath Freedom's sky;
    No more shall brave men wearily
Tramp to the music of a battle-cry.
    Resting, we dwell in peace, the hard fight o'er,
    Yet true to God and country evermore.

OUR DEAREST AND BEST WE GIVE UNTO THEE.

Yes, unto Thee we give to-day
   Our most-beloved one;
But, dearest Lord, we cannot say
   "Thy Holy Will be done!"

Most cherished hopes have fallen low,
   And crushed and broken lie
Upon the bier, where sad tears flow
   And dreams unfinished fade and die.

"He giveth His beloved sleep!"
   A sleep so free from earthly pain,
That even while bitterly we weep
   We would not have him wake again.

Slowly the daylight fades away,
   And faintly glows the dying sun:
Lo! kneeling at Thy Feet, we pray,
   "Thy Holy Will be done!"

TO LONGFELLOW'S PICTURE.

Look gently on us, with the earnest, speaking eyes
  That saw so much of loveliness in all thy kind!
That gazed beyond the clouds for smiling skies,
  And in the present left the dead past far behind.
Wild passion did not sway the willing pen
  Which never faltered in thy tireless hand,
But toiled with love for suffering fellow-men,
  And aimed to make earth's brief life fair and grand.

And who shall say the labor was all vain
  In which a long and blameless life was spent?
Ah! not the hearts oppressed with bitter pain,
  For whom his wise and cheering words were meant.
Sad tears may fall, some thoughts will bring
  Hushed memories from the past's long-folded leaves,
But hope has balm for sorrow's ache and sting,
  And consolation when the human spirit grieves.

We know that if the long-sealed lips could speak
  The loving heart would prompt him still to say,
If he had helped to guide the frail and weak,
  Or taught a faithless, wandering heart to pray,
His hours of mortal life had been well spent
  And his long-cherished visions well fulfilled;
That talents by an all-wise Master lent
  Had been made use of as the keeper willed.

.

Though worthier lips than ours have sung his praise,
    We lay a loving tribute at his feet:
We too must have our share of dreary days,
    But soon or late the dark and sunshine meet;
And for the courage which his teachings give,
    And for the skill and patience of his art,
We love him, and his songs shall live
    Re-echoing in the human heart.

TO ST. CATHARINE OF ALEXANDRIA.

Not for thy far-famed beauty, and the power
   Which might have crowned thy happiness on earth,
   The honored and historic house which gave thee birth,
The rare and brilliant charms which were thy dower,—
   But for the meek humility which laid
All honor and all worldly wealth aside,
   We love thee, Alexandria's fair maid,
And claim thee for our patroness and guide.

The world holds us in thrall—our trembling feet
   Pace restlessly on its alluring strands,
   And with unseeing eyes we place our hands
On treasures that a mortal life deems sweet.
   We strive for dreams that quickly pass away
And leave but little trace to mark their reign
   When summer's richer bloom succeeds to May,
And life bears many scars of grief and pain.

Pure virgin heart! in which Love's burning glow
   Supplanted all that worldly lives desire;
   Oh! meek self-sacrifice, which placed within that fire
The vanity and pomp of things below:
   O chosen spouse of Christ! whose virtues shine
Undimmed through passing ages, pray that we
May imitate thy burning love, thy sweet humility,
   May keep our hearts as meek and pure as thine!

MUSIC.

(To one who loves her art better than herself.)

Our great Creator, mindful of inconstant hearts—
 Clinging at times to heaven, but most to earth—
Designed, of boundless love for men, the arts
 Which lead us to a higher, nobler birth.
We read the words long-quiet hands have penned,
 And find beneath the lessons they contain;
The writers' lives have reached a fruitful end,
 But their abiding faith and hope remain.

We stand before a picture, musing on the dreams
 That wrapped the artist's soul in days forever fled,
And on the glowing canvas wandering memory seems
 To trace the thoughts he painted as the quiet hours
  sped.
The sculptor's hand has formed of senseless clay
 Fair visions of a noble soul's ideal,
And though he sleeps well after life's brief day
 His works have power to make us think and feel.

And if we wish to lay aside the cares
 That vex our troubled souls from time to time,
To breathe out all our weariness in prayers
 Worthy with heaven's angelic choirs to chime,
Our loving fingers touch the pliant keys,
 And play with lingering tenderness the strains
That soothe the restless heart to tranquil ease,
 And care and turmoil vanish—happiness remains. .

All moods are here:—the cry of mad despair
    That goes out from a wrecked and wasted life;
The bitterness of poverty and care;
    The recklessness of passion and of strife.
Long, long ago, a master fierce with pain
    Touched the responsive chords in speechless grief,
And told through them the love that was in vain—
    The dream of joy whose reign had been too brief.

And some have sat, with lowly drooping head,
    Caressing the white keys through bitter tears,
Recalling words and memories of the dead,
    Which love intensifies with passing years.
But that same bitterness has passed away,
    Leaving a quiet sadness in its stead;
" Hope on," we hear angelic voices say;
    "'Tis well with your beloved and happy dead."

Who has not known the grief, the hopes and fears,
    The joy of happy moments, felt by all,
Revealed to the loved instrument in far-off years,
    Whose melodies still hold the world in thrall?
Through mighty strains we dream of wealth and power,
    Of honors bravely won and grandly worn;
Through solemn strains, of life's fast-fleeting hour,
    And happy hearts of earthly grandeur shorn;

And as a sweet, low strain falls softly o'er us,
   We see no more the paths by mortals trod,
For we behold a place more fair before us,
   And then, ah! then, we dream of heaven, and God.
And should it be our happy lot to cast
   On even the least of His one ray of sun,
Oh! let us serve Him ere the day has passed,
   And the long night-time's endless rest begun.

IN THE PEACE PAST UNDERSTANDING.

Who that has seen the brightness of her smile,
    And listened to her words, so calm and kind—
Who that has pondered thoughtfully a while
    On the sweet charity of her broad Christian mind,
Can turn from the drear void her absence makes
    Without one bitter tear—one vain regret?
For memory once-joyous harp-strings wakes,
    And dwells on chords we gladly would forget.

Brave and unselfish to the last,
    She smiled in the old way again,
And one more honored life had passed
    From all earth's grief, its care and pain.
Aye! heap her bier with flowers, their fragrant bloom
    Speaks of a life that never dies—
A life beyond the silent tomb,
    Smiling from God's immortal skies.

A crown to-day rewards a cross;
    Its heavenly brightness gleams,
And pierces through our bitter loss,
    With hope in all its beams.
So beautiful and calm to-day,
    Serenely on God's loving breast,
With all her fierce pain soothed away,
    She sleeps in love and rest!

21

Oh! winter snows, fall soft and white
　　Upon that dearly cherished mound ;
Oh ! fair spring blossoms, fragile, bright,
　　Within its loved precincts abound ;
Oh ! fragrant summer roses, blow
　　And fall o'er it in showers,
For she who calmly sleeps below
　　Is one of heaven's flowers !

SIC TRANSIT GLORIA MUNDI.

A few swift-passing years,
Well marked by smiles and tears,
And hiding in their folded leaves
Sweet fancies playful childhood weaves;
The golden dreams of life's brief May,
The waking of a later day,
And long-dead thoughts that Evening brings
On Memory-laden wings.

Days when the sunbeams stray
Upon our merry way,
And days when even heaven's clear blue
Is shrouded from our mortal view;
When thorns have sprung in mid-day hours
In paths that Morning decked with flowers,
And gloomy shadows over all
Our hopes in silence fall.

The cherished friends of old
Now lying 'neath the mold ;
The eyes whose loving glances stayed
Our bitter words when passion swayed ;
The hands whose light touch spurred us 'on,
Forever missed, forever gone :
Ah ! Heaven must be very fair,
For those we love are there.

We dry the bitter tears
That fall o'er buried years,
And I turn towards the smiling skies
So far above our weary eyes.
Oh ! Earth, when thy vain idols fall,
One hope remains to comfort all:
Of our fond hopes the dearest, best—
In Heaven, there is rest !

THREE FRIENDS OF MINE.

The last October sun had set,
  Leaving the night which young hearts give to
    mirth,
When we four happy girl friends met
  To have "the gayest time on earth!"
Four very different girls, in truth,
  Made the old house with laughter gay;
Alike in this much—love and youth
  Were theirs, and care was far away.

Describe them ?   Well, I'll try my best
  To do them justice—three of them ;
The fourth I beg to leave at rest,
  You know her very well as "Em ;"
The other three were Marys ; strange
  So vast a difference marked their ways ;
Yet, after all, I would not change
  These friends, so worthy of my praise.

One Mary has the clear gray eyes
  Whose power I have learned to know;
Such dazzling brightness in them lies
  You scarce can read the depths below.
Brown ringlets fall caressingly,
  As though they loved their resting-place,
And lend, if such a thing could be,
  An added sweetness to her face.

An airy and coquettish way
    Suits this friend well, yet hides from view,
Beneath a manner light and gay,
    A heart and nature warm and true.
Don't change, dear Mary! each caprice
    Belongs by every right to you;
And if your many moods should cease,
    I might not love you as I do.

Oh! Mary of the trusting heart,
    The world holds you unspoiled and sweet;
You still believe the better part
    That may be found in those you meet.
I would not have you lose that trust
    Which seems so much a part of you;
And when youth fades, as fade it must,
    Believe, dear, still that hearts are true.

Grave, honest brown eyes mark the third
    Of these dear friends; almost a child,
Whom pain and doubt have never stirred,
    And on whom life has always smiled.
An honest mind that scorns deceit,
    A heart to friendship ever true;
Ah! sister mine, it were not meet .
    That I should ask a change in you.

You think I am most strangely blest
   In having friends like these to claim?
Well, if the truth must be confessed,
   Believe me that I think the same.
But sometimes those who deeply feel
   Too seldom can express it well,
And all their hearts would fain reveal
   Their lips have little power to tell.

SYMPATHY.

Standing upon the height which you have won
    Through struggles with your passion and your will,
Gaze downward—with the contest just begun,
    Your brothers slowly mount the rugged hill.
Ah! do not scorn the least, remembering
    That Wisdom's Hand has fashioned weak and strong,
Or, with a cold contempt and pity, fling
    Your hard-bought conquest at another's wrong.

They are so few, the years we spend on earth,
    So full of thought of worldly loss and gain,
We scarce can learn our fellow-creatures' worth,
    The nobler nature that the humblest lives contain.
And so we keep the little words of praise,
    Which add new joy to joy, and lessen care,
Deep in our hearts, forgetting weary days
    Through sympathy grow easier to bear.

In the full knowledge that divinely over all
    God watches, and His Will does not decree
That even the weakest step should faint or fall
    In the long pathway to a glad eternity,
We live and hope; oh! may that knowledge bring
    Patience and love for every passing day:
So helping, trusting, heart to heart shall cling
    In perfect love, that knows of no decay.

HYMN TO ST. CATHARINE.

Beneath far Eastern skies,
   Where vice held regal sway,
First shone the light that lies
   Upon the world to-day.

Not as the glaring sun
   That dazzles with its beams,
And when the day is done
   Fades into crimson streams,

But with diviner light,
   That luring not with gold
Still shines through all our night,
   And leaves no dark, no cold.

Oh ! chosen spouse of God,
   Let thy bright radiance fill
The weary pathways trod
   By erring creatures still.

And when our lives shall cease,
   Of earth no more a part,
Guide us to rest and peace
   Within His Sacred Heart.

REQUIESCAT.

When tired eyes have closed on earthly scenes,
　And weary feet to fairer paths have strayed,
We, but half-knowing what the silence means,
　And seeing only darkness, are afraid.
Yet, what is death, that we must shrink in fear?
　And what life, that we cling to it so long?
Ah! one makes pain and grief forever clear,
　And one is but a conflict for the strong.

Yet we have loved, dear Lord; Thou wilt not chide
　If we forget that Thou didst bear a cross,
If our weak tears in falling sometimes hide
　The light which Thou art shedding on our loss.
Oh! teach us that the mist has fallen now
　From the young eyes that fondly gaze on Thee,
And help us 'neath Thy Will to firmly bow,
　Not in dumb sorrow, but in faith, and willingly,

IN MEMORIAM.

Who lives for God alone shall die in Him,
  And know His rest and peace.   Oh ! weary hearts,
Oh ! eyes with care and sorrow dim,
  All our unceasing restlessness departs,
When, at the silent touch of the Unseen,
  We give our mortal lives into His care,
Unasking what eternity may mean,
  In full content to know that God is there.

Therefore, no vain tears fall upon our dead :
  Why should we weep, though every gentle word
Which once was ours to claim is left unsaid ?
  The voice we loved, on this low earth unheard,
Makes music in a home more fair and bright ;
  Grief would be selfish, tears but weak and vain,
Remembering our darkness is her light,
  And our brief parting her eternal gain.

A PICTURE.

The clear Easter sunlight is streaming
  In gladness and brightness o'er all,
And I—I am standing and dreaming
  Where most of its light seems to fall,
      Touching up into glory the poets, who sleep
      After toil, in a rest that is tranquil and deep.

And, lo ! I am gazing no more
  On the pictured resemblance of men,
For the days which they lived in of yore
  I have brought back in fancy again ;
      All the glad Easter sunlight has faded away,
      And I am in far-off New England to-day.

In old Massachusetts, the trees
  Are just bursting to bloom, but the birds
Have ceased to pour forth on the breeze
  Their rejoicing ; they list to the words
      Of the poet of Nature, who walks with hushed tread,
      Drinking in the deep calm of the skies overhead.

With head lowly bowed in deep thought,
  I see Concord's learned sage stand,
And each precious moment is fraught
  With dreams that will float o'er the land :
      Ah ! the dreams that he cherished—dreams born
                    amid flowers—
      We have but to long for—to seek—they are ours.

In the calm after-tide of a life
  That is worthy of hearing " Well done,"
Deep scarred with the bitterest strife,
  One rests, with his honors hard won !
    And his gray head is heaped with the prayers of
      the slave
    Whom he called in truth, " Brother," and labored to
      save.

There is laughter more frequent than tears,
  Where the Autocrat pauses a while ;
And often in long-after years
  The moan will be checked in the smile,
    When the hand that is guiding the tired pen to-day
    Has completed its task, and has mouldered away.

Shall one more low voice strive to speak
  Of him who is greatest and best ?
Ah ! no, for my words are too weak,
  And his undying fame does not rest
    On the tributes of others ; he speaks, we are mute,
    And but one perfect melody strays from the lute.

And lastly, the teacher and guide
  Of the weary, and sinful, and worn ;
As softly I come to his side
  His voice on the calm breeze is borne,
    And I listen intently, my eyes growing dim,
    For one word, one only, to cherish from him

Whose lessons of wisdom and truth
　　Oft guided my faltering pen ;
Oh ! bard of the love of my youth,
　　I bring you my homage again,
　　　　And the old-time sweet patience and courage I see
　　　　In the eyes which so gently are gazing on me.

And this is my question to-day,
　　As each beautiful record I trace,
Oh ! as the long years pass away,
　　Will one word of mine merit a place
　　　　In some world-weary heart, dreaming on through
　　　　　the cold
　　　　Of a day that the sunlight will turn into gold ?

GREETING TO REV. GERALD P. COGHLAN.

How calm and cold our written words will look
  When we have placed our thoughts beneath their
    guise!
Lo! as try to frame them, memory's book
  Discloses all its treasures to our eyes.
What does its record show? The happy days
  So lightly prized, when all their golden store
Of Nature's rarest gifts made bright the ways
  To which our lives shall lead us back no more.

And through those memories one name we trace
  So often, that we turn in eager quest
To find what claims for it so large a place,
  And why its gleam is brighter than the rest.
Look well; no wondrous deeds—a gentle word,
  Said lightly, and perhaps with little thought;
Said and forgotten, but the hearts it stirred
  Cherished the memory of the good it wrought.

To-day, when many loyal hearts have come,
  In glowing praise their mighty love to speak,
Why should our erstwhile ready lips be dumb,
  Though faint our speech, and poor our words and
    weak?
And yet, what need has that calm life of praise,
  On which God smiling stretches out His Hand,
And gives His benediction to the ways
  Whose heights of love we cannot understand?

Far, far from things of earth we lift our eyes,
  And dimly see, so fast the shadows fall,
The goal we seek, whose shining gateway lies
  Adown the path which has an end for all.
Beyond the mist, so bright the radiant gleam
  That trials are scarce worthy of record,
And sorrow grows an unremembered dream
  Before the message, "God is thy reward!"

Father! our voices fail; the past has fled,
  We cannot keep its pleasures at our will,
But, though our loving words are coldly said,
  We claim to be your faithful children still;
And as such pray that all the kindliness
  You give to other lives unceasingly,
May be returned with strengthened power to bless—
  That as your worth so may your merit be!

THE PARTING OF THE WAYS.

I feared to raise my eyes, lest I should see
That not far off our paths would separate;
I was content—ah! too content—to wait,
    And let the happy days pass quietly,
As they had done so long: I might have known
    That He, whose Love goes on eternally,
Would claim that young life in its purity
    Ere adverse winds across its course had blown,

And drifted it through all the bitter pain,
The weariness, the misty doubts and fears
Which are the world's; where, after many years,
    We learn to count the cost of what is vain,
And scornful that we saw it not before,
    And that earth's faded beauty looked so fair,
We turn at last to God, giving Him little more
    Than broken hearts for all His love and care.

My dearest! I am standing here alone,
Gazing through tears far down the quiet way
Which is your wise choice now, and oh! to-day
    I have not strength to follow out my own,
Which looks so dark, so dark, and strange, and cold
    Without the smile which, at my slightest word,
Springing to life, in low-breathed message told
    Of thoughts with which the childish heart was
        stirred:

Childish in one thing only, that no trace
Was on it of the world of doubt and sin,
And all the child's sweet innocence within
    Reflected on the pure and noble face,
And spoke from out the deep, dark eyes, whose gaze
    Seemed fitted more for things of heavenly birth
Than that it should grow troubled in the ways,
    The sad and time-worn, toil-worn ways of earth!

Hers was a nature few could understand;
One which in contemplation of her Lord
Forbore the careless smile, the bitter word,
    And seeing all souls noble made demand
For something greater, worthier of us all
    Than we had thought to give. She had a gentle
        way
Of smiling into silence comment small,
    And making natures nobler for her sway.

I miss the steady hand which always led,
In spite of years, where it was best to go,
And oh! far more than all, the bright smile's glow
    Which o'er my life its richest fullness shed.
And at the cross-roads, where her loving eyes
    Look last on me, then bravely looked before,
I stand forlornly as the daylight dies,
    Longing for that which shall be mine no more.

LIGHT.

A little child, who spoke of Things Divine
    As though she moved amidst them every day,
Laid her white hand with gentle touch on mine,
    Eager to charm my quiet mood away.

I sat with half-closed eyes, and only felt
    As in a dream the baby presence near;
My thoughts, which through the long, sad day had
      dwelt
    On all that made the vanished past so dear,

Had with the falling darkness turned to Him
    Whose Love I had not claimed when it was day;
Now, with a heavy heart, and eyes grown dim,
    I saw my brightest visions die away.

Ungrateful! oh! ungrateful; all my years
    Have felt in every joy His love for me,
And only when my smiles have changed to tears,
    I thank Him for His mercy willingly.

"What are you thinking of?" The baby head
    Was drooping, and the voice was very low;
The child's sad wonder roused me, and I said,
    "Of what Heaven is, my darling, do you know?"

Was it a child of earth? Ah! could it be?
    Who, with a far-off smile, and eyes grown bright,
Stood there beside me, and so reverently
    Said, "Yes, I do know; *Heaven is light!*"

ODE

For the Silver Jubilee of the Cathedral T. A. B. Society.

The scorn of those
Whose only love is self—who cannot see
The kindred spirit of humanity,
    Was what you chose.
He was your model whose Divine Hand's touch
Had blessed the poor and outcast willingly:
Lo! hear His voice through ages, "Inasmuch
As to the least, ye do it unto Me!"

Sorrow and sin had grown
So common that the great world passed them by,
Hearing unmoved, or with regretful sigh,
    The orphan's bitter moan,
Which told of aching hearts, of tears that fell
From childish eyes, where Fancy's magic spell
Had never lighted; from which hate and gloom
Looked on the joys that happy children know,
And learned too soon to view the awful doom
Which filled their lives with poverty and woe.

God saw and planned:
He looked into the faithful hearts where dwelt
The great and boundless charity which felt
    His mercy would demand,
One day, of them the efforts they had made
To rend the fair disguise which Sin had worn;
Who knew He blessed the hand stretched out in aid,
The lips that smiled when others curled in scorn.

Thus was the work begun:
And Truth's steep mountain, though so hard to
    climb,
Draws many to it in God's own good time.
    Ah! what the years have done—
The tears that changed to smiles, the lives made
    blest,
Because you have so nobly led the way,
And smoothed it for your followers to-day—
Frail hands shall not record; God knows all best.

    Reverently linger o'er
The records of the past; the good deeds done,
The battles bravely fought, the triumphs won,
    By those now gone before,
Who stand within the radiant light of day,
Forgetful that their weary feet once pressed
The paths so hard to tread. All passed away
The toiling, and how calm and sweet the rest!
So shall your merit be, who love all men:
May He, who guards as well the high and low,
Give you the strength to do, the grace to know,
Till His Recording Angel writes, "Amen!"

MY DARTHEA.

There is no wondrous beauty in thy face,
Whose dear charm lies not in well-rounded grace,
    In faultless curve, or perfect symmetry ;
Thy sweetness from the world's cold glance is hid,
Yet in all graciousness it comes unbid
    For love or sympathy.

Grief which has hardened some, embittered more,
Has left thy nature gentler than before :
    Dost thou know how the smile which hides thy pain
Has shamed to rest much useless murmuring,
For what the years again may never bring—
    So weak, so vain ?

They call thee proud and cold who do not know
How wonderful, how tender is the glow
    Which lights those dear, dear eyes, whene'er they rest
In steadfast gaze on what, of all we view
Is grandest, noblest, worthiest of you—
    The beautiful, the best!

I am content to hear thy slightest word,
To see thee smile, to feel thy touch has stirred
    Thoughts into life none other can impart;
My love is far too deep to give thee praise,
But, Darthea, for all thy gentle ways,
    Take thou my heart.

THE HIGHEST ART.

Far on the distant hill I saw the light,
And struggled on, though many fell asleep;
It was a long and lonely watch to keep,
So bleak the way, so coldly still the night!
Ah! me, the load-star faded from my sight,
And I too rested, but it was to weep:
"Alas!" I said, "the ascent is so steep,
I will return, and none shall mark my flight:"
I saw deep down into a great man's heart,
And mourned the wounds a slighting world had
     made;
He smiled in answering, "Forbear thy ruth,
And journey on; thy sorrow shall depart,
Thy soul find peace, and be no more afraid:
Thus love rewards the search for endless Truth."

TO ALICE.

The world sees many faults in those
  Whose pleasure chiefly lies in books,
But, child, their lover early grows
  To smile at its averted looks.
How worthless seem the gilded ways
  Through which men wander blindly on,
To one who, all unmindful, strays
  With those whose light still shines upon
The passing ages! Willingly
  Forego the idle waste of hours
Which some call life; this company
  Rewards disciples well, and dowers
With richest life those brave to scale
  The thorn-set mountain. Childish eyes,
Look calmly up! No glittering veil
  Of hollow pretense can disguise
The joy which you will find at last.
  So, bravely take the path well-trod,
And, with weak terrors fought, temptatious
    passed,
  Your soul shall grow more pleasing unto God.

ALONE.

A quiet spot, where few would find their way;
May sunlight on an old and broken stone,
A grave by sweet wild-flowers overgrown,
Whose fragrance breathes of life, and not decay;
And, pitiful it seems, a rose, full-blown,
Half-hides beneath its leaves one word, "Alone."
Has fancy changed the cloudless sky to gray,
Or do we see the sun through tears to-day?
Oh, silent heart! I wonder if you know
What hands caress the flowers above your head,
By whom this long-neglected path is trod?
I wonder was it all so long ago
That you forget the lonely life you led,
Enraptured in the presence of your God?

LAST DAYS.

A new hope dawns upon the Summer now,
    And sad delight the heart of Nature stirs;
The sweetest of the months, with calm, fair brow,
    Is crowning brows as fair and calm as hers.

Oh, children, watching from a magic land,
    Whose brightness lends the world a tender glow,
Fame, wealth, and happiness at your command,
    Would that the years to come might leave you so!

Yes, linger now; these days bring to a close
    The glory of your childhood, fleeting fast;
Awhile in paths of peace the calm brook flows,
    But reaches wind and storm at last, at last!

Ah, will life seem too hard when sorrow's crown
    Lies heavy on the brows that flowers adorn?
Will you smile on, or lay the burden down
    As one too heavy to be meekly borne?

How your last school-days vividly recall
    A happy child, whose heart was just as light,
Who felt that faith and love were dear to all,
    Whose tears blot out the shattered dream to-night.

Your passing footsteps slowly die away,
    And on the summer wind there comes to me
The faint; sweet music of a far-off day,
    Vibrating on the chords of Memory.